MW00488536

THIS FUCKING JOURNAL BELONGS TO:

_____

Published by Sourcebooks
P.O. Box 4410, Naperville, Illinois 60567-4410
(630) 961-3900
sourcebooks.com

Printed and bound in China.
OGP 10 9 8 7 6 5 4 3

CARPE FUCKING DIEM

A JOURNAL TO
SEIZE THE FUCKING DAY

 sourcebooks

WELL, TIME TO

GET

FUCKING

STARTED

ANOTHER FUCKING LIST...

MAKE
TODAY
YOUR
BITCH!

YOU

FUCKING

GOT

THIS

— / — / —

LIVE,
LAUGH,
LEAVE ME
THE FUCK
ALONE.

ANOTHER FUCKING LIST...

C'EST LA

FUCKING

VIE

LOVE IS SHIT.
GET DONUTS.

ANOTHER FUCKING LIST...

MAKE TODAY YOUR BITCH!

BREATHE

OUT THE

BULLSHIT

—/—/—

QUICK NOTE:
TRUST
NO ONE.

— / — / —

SAVE
THE TREES
AND SHIT.

ANOTHER FUCKING LIST...

MAKE
TODAY
YOUR
BITCH!

FRESH

OUT OF

FUCKS

— / — / —

SEIZE THE FUCKING DAY.

ANOTHER FUCKING LIST...

MAKE
TODAY
YOUR
BITCH!

BITCH,

PLEASE.

— / — / —

NOTE TO
SELF:
DON'T BE
SHITTY.

ANOTHER FUCKING LIST...

MAKE
TODAY
YOUR
BITCH!

FANCY

AS

FUCK

**GO EAT SOME
FUCKING ICE CREAM.**

CAN YOU
FUCKING
NOT?

ANOTHER FUCKING LIST...

MAKE
TODAY
YOUR
BITCH!

FUCK.

THAT.

NOISE.

—— / —— / ——

START YOUR
IDGAF DIET.

ANOTHER FUCKING LIST...

MAKE
TODAY
YOUR
BITCH!

OH

HOT

DAMN.

— / — / —

EYE ROLL

ANOTHER FUCKING LIST...

MAKE
TODAY
YOUR
BITCH!

- [x] LIKE
- [x] A
- [x] FUCKING
- [x] BOSS

— / — / —

SOUNDS
BATSHIT
CRAZY.

SORRY IF I
LOOKED
INTERESTED.
I'M NOT.

ANOTHER FUCKING LIST...

MAKE
TODAY
YOUR
BITCH!

OH,

FOR FUCK'S SAKE...

— / — / —

ANOTHER FUCKING LIST...

MAKE TODAY YOUR BITCH!

FAN-

FUCKING-

TASTIC...

FUCK IT,
PASS THE
CHEESE.

LOL,
OKAY
BITCH.

ANOTHER FUCKING LIST...

MAKE TODAY YOUR BITCH!

GET.

SHIT.

DONE.

— / — / —

FUCKING
TREAT
YO' SELF.

THANKFUL
AS FUCK.

ANOTHER FUCKING LIST...

MAKE
TODAY
YOUR
BITCH!

IT'S

FUCKING

LIT

—/—/—

TIME TO MAKE
SHIT HAPPEN.

ANOTHER FUCKING LIST...

MAKE TODAY YOUR BITCH!

BASIC

BITCH

SEASON

RAY OF
FUCKING
SUNSHINE.

CLOUDY
WITH A CHANCE
OF BULLSHIT.

ANOTHER FUCKING LIST...

MAKE
TODAY
YOUR
BITCH!

NOT TODAY
SATAN

UGH.

**LONG LIVE THE
RESTING BITCH FACE.**

ANOTHER FUCKING LIST...

MAKE
TODAY
YOUR
BITCH!

A CONSTANT

FUCKING

DELIGHT

WHAT KIND
OF FUCKERY
IS THIS?

—/—/—

ANOTHER FUCKING LIST...

MAKE
TODAY
YOUR
BITCH!

BITCH MODE

ACTIVATED

—/—/—

GTFO
AND GET
SOME DAMN
SUNSHINE.

ANOTHER FUCKING LIST...

MAKE
TODAY
YOUR
BITCH!

WHAT A

CLUSTERFUCK

BULLSHIT,
BULLSHIT,
AND MORE
BULLSHIT.

NOPE.
NOT
TODAY.

ANOTHER FUCKING LIST...

MAKE
TODAY
YOUR
BITCH!

ABSO**FUCKIN**LUTELY

*STARES
BLANKLY*

ANOTHER FUCKING LIST...

MAKE
TODAY
YOUR
BITCH!

KINDLY

FUCK

OFF...

FUCKING
TRY AGAIN
NEXT YEAR.

YOU'RE

FUCKING

DONE.

(HOORAY.)

NOTES AND SHIT...

NOTES AND SHIT...